Creative Company Direct 11/17/07 $27 L°

THE STORY OF THE
LOS ANGELES
CLIPPERS

CREATIVE EDUCATION

Published by Creative Education
123 South Broad Street
Mankato, Minnesota 56001
Creative Education is an imprint of The Creative Company.

DESIGN AND PRODUCTION BY **EVANSDAY DESIGN**

PHOTOGRAPHS BY Associated Press, AP, Getty Images (Bill Baptist / NBAE,
Andrew D. Bernstein / NBAE, Vince Bucci / AFP, Jim Cummins / NBAE,
Scott Cunningham, Stephen Dunn / Allsport, Stephen Dunn / NBAE,
Jonathan Ferrey, Focus on Sport, JEFF HAYNES / AFP, David McNew,
Anthony Neste / Time Life Pictures, Richard Pilling, Mike Powell /
NBAE, Wen Roberts / NBAE, Ron Turenne / NBAE), SportsChrome

LIBRARY OF CONGRESS CATALOGING-IN-PUBLICATION DATA

Frisch, Aaron.
The story of the Los Angeles Clippers / by Aaron Frisch.
p. cm. — (The NBA—a history of hoops)
Includes index.
ISBN-13: 978-1-58341-410-1
1. Los Angeles Clippers (Basketball team)—History—
Juvenile literature. I. Title. II. Series.

GV884.52.L65F75 2006
796.323'64'0979494—dc22   2005051415

First edition

9 8 7 6 5 4 3 2 1

COVER PHOTO: *Shaun Livingston*

THE STORY OF THE
LOS ANGELES
CLIPPERS

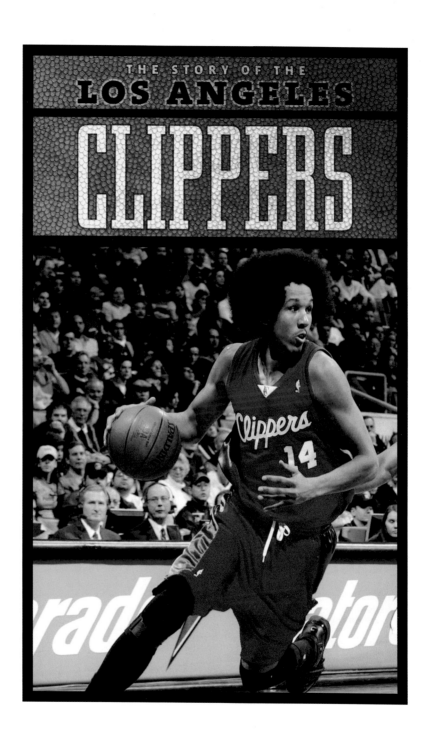

AARON FRISCH

CREATIVE C EDUCATION

As the last seconds

TICK OFF THE ARENA CLOCK, THE SMATTERING OF FANS
THROUGHOUT STAPLES CENTER APPLAUD THEIR TEAM'S
FINAL EFFORT OF THE SEASON. THE PLAYERS IN THE RED-
AND-WHITE UNIFORMS WITH THE CURSIVE LETTERING LOOK
UP AT THE SCOREBOARD AS THEY UNTUCK THEIR JERSEYS
AND TRUDGE SOLEMNLY TOWARD THE LOCKER ROOM. ON
THE BACKS OF THE JERSEYS ARE NAMES SUCH AS BRAND,
MAGGETTE, AND LIVINGSTON, BUT THEY COULD BE ALMOST
ANY NAMES FROM A HISTORY OF THREE AND A HALF DECADES.
THERE WILL BE NO PLAYOFFS FOR THE CLIPPERS, BUT THERE
IS ALWAYS NEXT YEAR....

BRAVE BEGINNINGS

LOS ANGELES, CALIFORNIA, IS ONE OF AMERICA'S largest cities. Founded in 1781 as a small Spanish mission, Los Angeles came under the United States' control in 1847 and grew rapidly. People were drawn to the city by its many attractive features, including its pleasant climate and beautiful nearby beaches and mountains.

Today, Los Angeles is known as the movie and television capital of the world. It is also known as something of a professional sports mecca. Many teams have settled in Los Angeles, including a National Basketball Association (NBA) team called the Clippers. The team settled in "L.A." in 1984, but its road to Los Angeles was a long and winding one.

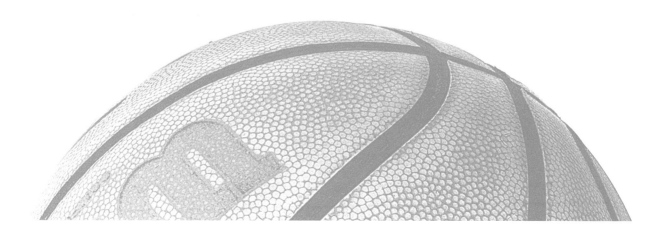

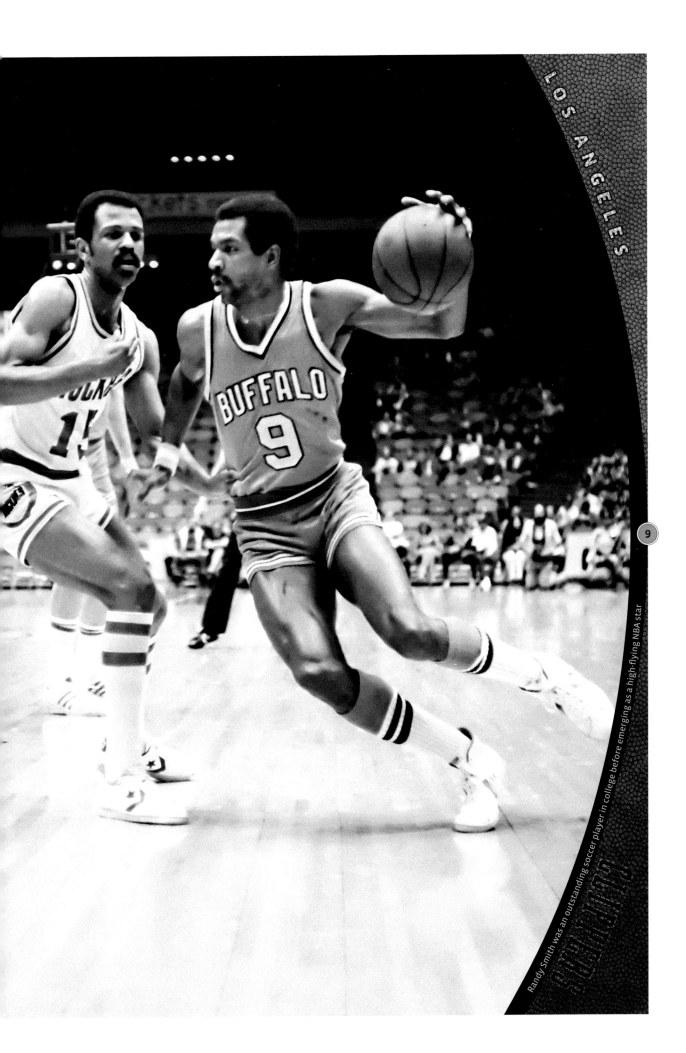

9

Randy Smith was an outstanding soccer player in college before emerging as a high-flying NBA star

Hall-of-Famer Jack Ramsay led the Braves to the playoffs in three of his four seasons as head coach

NBA

The Clippers started out across the country, in Buffalo, New York, as a team called the Braves. The Braves joined the NBA in 1970, and although they lost a lot of games their first few seasons, fans enjoyed some terrific performances by high-scoring center Bob Kauffman and young guard Randy Smith.

Even though Smith stood only 6-foot-3, he sometimes played forward because he was such a great leaper. Combining that leaping ability with amazing speed, Smith emerged as a top-notch defender and scorer. "I hate guarding him," admitted New York Knicks guard Walt Frazier. "Even when he isn't scoring, he's running so fast all over the place, and I have to chase him."

The Braves added an even more explosive star in 1972 by drafting center Bob McAdoo. The 6-foot-10 McAdoo netted 18 points a game as a rookie and grew more dominant in the seasons that followed, leading the league in scoring for three straight years. McAdoo never saw a shot he didn't like, putting the ball up from anywhere on the court with great accuracy.

MARVELOUS BOB MCADOO

Perhaps the greatest player the Clippers can lay claim to is one of the first players in franchise history: Bob McAdoo. A center with the quickness and deft shooting touch of a guard, McAdoo starred for the Buffalo Braves for five seasons—four of them under the guidance of Jack Ramsay, one of the finest NBA coaches of the 1970s. In 1974–75, McAdoo led the league in scoring with 34.5 points a game, pulled down 14.1 rebounds a night, and captured NBA Most Valuable Player (MVP) honors... and a place among the game's brightest stars. "I used to think he took bad shots, but I've changed my mind," said Los Angeles Lakers star center Kareem Abdul-Jabbar. "Nobody takes shots from where McAdoo does and hits like he does."

Smith, McAdoo, and forward Jim McMillian led Buffalo to the playoffs in 1974, 1975, and 1976. But the Braves were never able to reach the NBA Finals. The main obstacle holding them back was the Boston Celtics, the league's most powerful team. The Braves clashed with the Celtics and lost in both the 1974 and 1976 playoffs.

Braves fans didn't know it yet, but they had just witnessed the club's glory years. In the seasons that followed, the team suffered a series of quick coaching changes, and McMillian and McAdoo were traded away in moves that disappointed fans. In 1976–77, young forward Adrian Dantley averaged 20 points per game and won the Rookie of the Year award. Remarkably, at the end of the season, he too was traded away.

THE MAN IN CHARGE

Since 1986, the everyday operation of the Clippers franchise has been the responsibility of a legendary NBA figure: Elgin Baylor. As a player for the Minneapolis and then Los Angeles Lakers in the 1950s and '60s, Baylor was the Michael Jordan of his day—an acrobatic, 6-foot-5 dynamo who could score almost at will. In 1960–61, he averaged almost 35 points and 20 rebounds a game! "Pound for pound, no one was ever as great as Elgin Baylor," said fellow Lakers forward Tommy Hawkins. Fourteen years after ending his Lakers career, Baylor moved across Los Angeles and joined the Clippers organization. By 2006, he had been the Clippers' vice president of basketball operations for 21 years—the longest tenure of any top executive in the NBA.

13

Famous for his unpredictable but accurate shots, Bob McAdoo also set the franchise record for career rebounds

THE SAN DIEGO YEARS

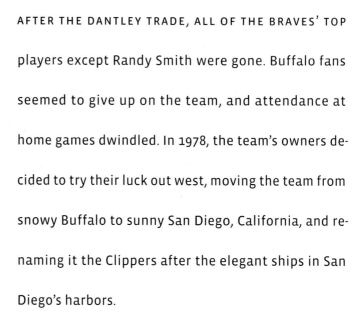

AFTER THE DANTLEY TRADE, ALL OF THE BRAVES' TOP players except Randy Smith were gone. Buffalo fans seemed to give up on the team, and attendance at home games dwindled. In 1978, the team's owners decided to try their luck out west, moving the team from snowy Buffalo to sunny San Diego, California, and renaming it the Clippers after the elegant ships in San Diego's harbors.

The Clippers were not particularly elegant at first, but fans enjoyed the heroics of crowd-pleasing guard Lloyd Free. Free, who later changed his name to World B. Free, was a colorful character and a flashy player who could score in bunches. In the team's first season in San Diego, his flamboyant—and frequent—shooting led the Clippers to a surprising 43–29 record. "People come right out of their seats when I do my thing," Free boasted. "People want to see that razzle-dazzle. They like seeing guys taking crazy shots and hitting them."

15

Offensive marvel Lloyd Free spent two seasons in San Diego, averaging more than 29 points a game

CLIPPERS

In 1984–85, point guard Norm Nixon became the team's first All-Star Game representative in five years

Before the next season, the Clippers made a major gamble, sending two players and a high draft pick to the Portland Trail Blazers for 6-foot-11 center Bill Walton. Just two years earlier, Walton—a San Diego native—had led the Blazers to an NBA championship and been named the league's MVP. But since that time, he had struggled with foot and knee injuries.

The gamble backfired badly. Injuries limited Walton to just 14 games in his first 3 seasons in a Clippers uniform, and San Diego—having invested a lot in the big center—fell to the bottom of the standings. "I'm personally responsible for the failure of the Clippers in San Diego," Walton would later admit.

San Diego showed flashes of potential the next few seasons. Young forward Terry Cummings was a bruising, high-scoring presence in the low post, and point guard Norm Nixon emerged as one of the league's best floor generals. Still, San Diego fans never really took to the Clippers, and in 1984, after just six seasons, the team headed north to Los Angeles.

The change of scenery did not mean a change of fortune, however. Cummings was sent to the Milwaukee Bucks in a poor trade, and Nixon suffered a leg injury that ended his career. Clippers fans wondered if things would ever change.

17

Center Bill Walton spent four seasons with the Clippers—three in San Diego and one in Los Angeles

NBA

THE DRAFT PICK THAT WASN'T

The Clippers had reason for optimism in the spring of 1989. They featured five players who had averaged more than 16 points per game the season before. They also had the second overall pick in the 1989 NBA Draft. The Clippers used the pick to select Danny Ferry, a 6-foot-10 forward who had starred at powerhouse Duke University. But Ferry stunned the league and outraged the Clippers by refusing to sign with the struggling Los Angeles franchise. The controversial decision, just the latest setback for the Clippers, seemed to hurt both sides: The Clippers stumbled throughout the 1990s, and Ferry—who played briefly in Italy before suiting up for two other NBA teams—put together a mediocre pro career, averaging 7 points and 2.8 rebounds a game over 13 seasons.

ANOTHER DIFFICULT DECADE

THE CLIPPERS HAD CAUGHT ONE LUCKY BREAK IN 1984, though. In that year's NBA Draft, they selected a hardworking forward named Michael Cage. Even though he could score when his team needed it, Cage prided himself most on his fierce rebounding and went after every loose ball as if his life depended on it. "[Hall of Fame center] Moses Malone told me that if you went after them all," Cage said, "one night you might get every rebound."

Cage never quite got every rebound, but he was a much-needed bright spot during some otherwise embarrassing years for the Clippers. In 1987–88, for example, Cage took a little of the sting off a 17–65 record by leading the NBA in rebounding with 13 boards per game. In spite of his heroics, Cage became part of an unsettling Clippers trend when he was traded to Seattle after that season.

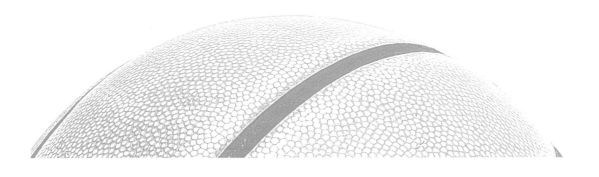

21

Michael Cage earned a reputation as one of the toughest and most durable players in the NBA

22

Danny Manning struggled with knee injuries but still became the third-leading scorer in Clippers history

In 1988, the Clippers again looked to the NBA Draft for their next star, using the first overall pick to take forward Danny Manning, who had almost single-handedly led the University of Kansas to the college national championship the year before. The Clippers assembled what looked like a talented lineup by putting Manning, forward Ken Norman, and versatile guard Ron Harper on the floor. But disaster struck when both Manning and Harper went down with knee injuries. It seemed that the Clippers were cursed.

Things finally looked brighter in old L.A. Sports Arena, the Clippers' home, in 1991. After going 31–51 during the 1990–91 season, Los Angeles made a coaching change, bringing in Larry Brown. The Clippers knew they were getting a proven winner; Brown had coached for 19 years in the college and professional ranks and posted just one losing season.

Brown did nothing to tarnish his reputation as a winner. In two seasons as the Clippers' leader, he led the club to the playoffs (and nearly playoff series victories) both times, breaking its 16-year postseason drought. Then, just as the team was making progress, Brown stepped down as coach. Manning, perhaps the team's best player, was also sent to Atlanta in a trade that worked out poorly. The Clippers were right back where they started—at the bottom.

BRENT BARRY, HIGH-FLYER

The mid-1990s were difficult years for the Clippers. But in 1996, a laid-back rookie named Brent "Bones" Barry gave them a welcome highlight. That year, Barry represented the Clippers in the NBA's annual Slam Dunk Contest. Expectations were low, especially when the gangly young forward took to the court for his turn without even removing his warm-up suit. But he threw down several impressive jams and then won the contest by running the length of the court and leaping from the free-throw line for the stuff. Some people found it significant that Barry was the first (and still only) white player to win the Slam Dunk title. "I was going to wear a 'White Men Can't Jump' T-shirt for the last dunk but thought better of it," the rookie joked afterwards.

25

The offensive output of Ken Norman (right) helped the Clippers earn playoff berths in 1992 and 1993

THE CLIPPERS SAIL ON

THE MID-1990S WERE MOSTLY UNEVENTFUL SEASONS in L.A. Sports Arena. A number of solid players—including forwards Loy Vaught and Lamond Murray and shot-blocking sensation Charles "Bo" Outlaw—wore Clippers jerseys during these years, but the team lacked a true star to take it to the next level. Typical of the Clippers' fortunes, a playoff appearance in 1997 was followed by a disastrous 17–65 record a year later.

The final years of the '90s and the first seasons of the 21st century were notable mostly for the revolving door of players the Clippers tried unsuccessfully to develop into stars. The club used the top overall pick in the 1998 NBA Draft to select center Michael Olowokandi, a player with raw skills but an appealing 7-foot-1 frame. Unfortunately, Olowokandi would never turn into the force the Clippers hoped for in five years with the club.

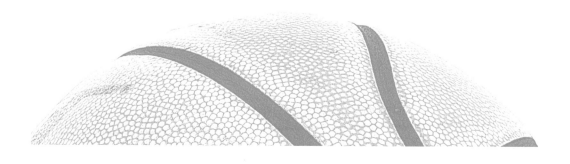

OUTLAW

45

With long arms and an explosive vertical leap, Bo Outlaw was a jaw-dropping dunker and shot blocker

Lamar Odom was amazing even as a rookie, leading the 1999–00 Clippers in points, assists and steals

Still, fans saw some exciting play during these years, thanks largely to such players as Lamar Odom. Standing 6-foot-10 and boasting effortless speed and ball-handling ability, Odom excelled at almost all positions. He also was skilled at putting the ball in the hands of such talented teammates as long-range marksman Eric Piatkowski. Unsurprisingly, however, Odom did not remain in a Los Angeles uniform for long. By the time he left town in 2003, the Clippers had posted 10 losing seasons in a row.

By the 2004–05 season, there was a new sense of hope among Clippers fans. Bigger crowds filled the new STAPLES Center—the team's home since 1999—to see the NBA's most ill-fated franchise put together a better record (37–45) than the rival Lakers for the first time in 12 years. Then, in 2005–06, the Clippers really opened eyes. Led by bruising forward Elton Brand, swingman Corey Maggette, speedy point guard Shaun Livingston, and veteran guard Sam Cassell, the team jumped to 47–35, beat the Denver Nuggets in the first round of the playoffs, and pushed the Phoenix Suns to seven games before falling in the second round. "It was a coming out party for myself and my teammates," said Brand, a fast-rising star. "We're only going to get better."

Although they have been represented by some of the game's finest players over the years, the Clippers have yet to claim an NBA championship. Tired of being overshadowed by their more successful crosstown rivals, the Lakers, today's Clippers are determined to put their legacy as perennial losers behind them and become L.A.'s featured attraction.

CLIPPER LUCK Most NBA teams suffer through occasional stretches in which their chances for success are undermined by injuries, trades that don't work out, or a lack of chemistry among teammates. Throughout the Clippers' history, this has been the norm rather than the exception. Twenty-one different head coaches have tried their hand at the helm of the Clippers, and although the team has featured many talented players, none stayed for long. Since joining the NBA more than 35 years ago, the Clippers franchise has yet to win a league, conference, or even division championship and has made the playoffs only seven times—winning just two playoff series. In 2000, Sports Illustrated called the Clippers "The worst franchise in sports history." Los Angeles fans hoped that the Clippers' inspired play in the 2006 playoffs was a sign that their luck was finally changing.

31

Behind forward Elton Brand, the Clippers came within one victory of the 2006 Western Conference Finals